PROSPECTS LOG

Contact & Initial Follow Up Tracker

This Prospects Log Belongs to:

FROM ____________ **TO** ______________

Published by Nevco Marketing
for ShowroomSalesSkills.com
ISBN: 978-1-989686-41-6

General Notes

PROSPECTS LOG

Name:
Date: Phone: Followup:

Name:
Date: Phone: Followup:

Name:
Date: Phone: Followup:

Name:
Date: Phone: Followup:

Name:
Date: Phone: Followup:

General Notes

PROSPECTS LOG

Name:
Date: Phone: Followup:

Name:
Date: Phone: Followup:

Name:
Date: Phone: Followup:

Name:
Date: Phone: Followup:

Name:
Date: Phone: Followup:

General Notes

PROSPECTS LOG

Name:
Date: Phone: Followup:

Name:
Date: Phone: Followup:

Name:
Date: Phone: Followup:

Name:
Date: Phone: Followup:

Name:
Date: Phone: Followup:

General Notes

PROSPECTS LOG

Name:

Date: Phone: Followup:

Name:

Date: Phone: Followup:

Name:

Date: Phone: Followup:

Name:

Date: Phone: Followup:

Name:

Date: Phone: Followup:

General Notes

PROSPECTS LOG

Name:
Date: Phone: Followup:

Name:
Date: Phone: Followup:

Name:
Date: Phone: Followup:

Name:
Date: Phone: Followup:

Name:
Date: Phone: Followup:

General Notes

PROSPECTS LOG

Name:

Date: Phone: Followup:

Name:

Date: Phone: Followup:

Name:

Date: Phone: Followup:

Name:

Date: Phone: Followup:

Name:

Date: Phone: Followup:

General Notes

PROSPECTS LOG

Name:

Date: Phone: Followup:

Name:

Date: Phone: Followup:

Name:

Date: Phone: Followup:

Name:

Date: Phone: Followup:

Name:

Date: Phone: Followup:

General Notes

PROSPECTS LOG

Name:

Date: Phone: Followup:

Name:

Date: Phone: Followup:

Name:

Date: Phone: Followup:

Name:

Date: Phone: Followup:

Name:

Date: Phone: Followup:

General Notes

PROSPECTS LOG

Name:
Date: Phone: Followup:

Name:
Date: Phone: Followup:

Name:
Date: Phone: Followup:

Name:
Date: Phone: Followup:

Name:
Date: Phone: Followup:

General Notes

PROSPECTS LOG

Name:

Date: Phone: Followup:

Name:

Date: Phone: Followup:

Name:

Date: Phone: Followup:

Name:

Date: Phone: Followup:

Name:

Date: Phone: Followup:

General Notes

PROSPECTS LOG

Name:

Date: Phone: Followup:

Name:

Date: Phone: Followup:

Name:

Date: Phone: Followup:

Name:

Date: Phone: Followup:

Name:

Date: Phone: Followup:

General Notes

PROSPECTS LOG

Name:
Date: Phone: Followup:

Name:
Date: Phone: Followup:

Name:
Date: Phone: Followup:

Name:
Date: Phone: Followup:

Name:
Date: Phone: Followup:

General Notes

PROSPECTS LOG

Name:

Date: Phone: Followup:

Name:

Date: Phone: Followup:

Name:

Date: Phone: Followup:

Name:

Date: Phone: Followup:

Name:

Date: Phone: Followup:

General Notes

PROSPECTS LOG

Name:

Date: Phone: Followup:

Name:

Date: Phone: Followup:

Name:

Date: Phone: Followup:

Name:

Date: Phone: Followup:

Name:

Date: Phone: Followup:

General Notes

PROSPECTS LOG

Name:
Date: Phone: Followup:

Name:
Date: Phone: Followup:

Name:
Date: Phone: Followup:

Name:
Date: Phone: Followup:

Name:
Date: Phone: Followup:

General Notes

PROSPECTS LOG

Name:
Date: Phone: Followup:

Name:
Date: Phone: Followup:

Name:
Date: Phone: Followup:

Name:
Date: Phone: Followup:

Name:
Date: Phone: Followup:

General Notes

PROSPECTS LOG

Name:

Date: Phone: Followup:

Name:

Date: Phone: Followup:

Name:

Date: Phone: Followup:

Name:

Date: Phone: Followup:

Name:

Date: Phone: Followup:

General Notes

PROSPECTS LOG

Name:

Date: Phone: Followup:

Name:

Date: Phone: Followup:

Name:

Date: Phone: Followup:

Name:

Date: Phone: Followup:

Name:

Date: Phone: Followup:

General Notes

PROSPECTS LOG

Name:
Date: Phone: Followup:

Name:
Date: Phone: Followup:

Name:
Date: Phone: Followup:

Name:
Date: Phone: Followup:

Name:
Date: Phone: Followup:

General Notes

PROSPECTS LOG

Name:
Date: Phone: Followup:

Name:
Date: Phone: Followup:

Name:
Date: Phone: Followup:

Name:
Date: Phone: Followup:

Name:
Date: Phone: Followup:

General Notes

PROSPECTS LOG

Name:

Date: Phone: Followup:

Name:

Date: Phone: Followup:

Name:

Date: Phone: Followup:

Name:

Date: Phone: Followup:

Name:

Date: Phone: Followup:

General Notes

PROSPECTS LOG

Name:

Date: Phone: Followup:

Name:

Date: Phone: Followup:

Name:

Date: Phone: Followup:

Name:

Date: Phone: Followup:

Name:

Date: Phone: Followup:

General Notes

PROSPECTS LOG

Name:

Date: Phone: Followup:

Name:

Date: Phone: Followup:

Name:

Date: Phone: Followup:

Name:

Date: Phone: Followup:

Name:

Date: Phone: Followup:

General Notes

PROSPECTS LOG

Name:

Date: Phone: Followup:

Name:

Date: Phone: Followup:

Name:

Date: Phone: Followup:

Name:

Date: Phone: Followup:

Name:

Date: Phone: Followup:

General Notes

PROSPECTS LOG

Name:

Date: Phone: Followup:

Name:

Date: Phone: Followup:

Name:

Date: Phone: Followup:

Name:

Date: Phone: Followup:

Name:

Date: Phone: Followup:

General Notes

PROSPECTS LOG

Name:
Date: Phone: Followup:

Name:
Date: Phone: Followup:

Name:
Date: Phone: Followup:

Name:
Date: Phone: Followup:

Name:
Date: Phone: Followup:

General Notes

PROSPECTS LOG

Name:
Date: Phone: Followup:

Name:
Date: Phone: Followup:

Name:
Date: Phone: Followup:

Name:
Date: Phone: Followup:

Name:
Date: Phone: Followup:

General Notes

PROSPECTS LOG

Name:

Date: Phone: Followup:

Name:

Date: Phone: Followup:

Name:

Date: Phone: Followup:

Name:

Date: Phone: Followup:

Name:

Date: Phone: Followup:

General Notes

PROSPECTS LOG

Name:
Date: Phone: Followup:

Name:
Date: Phone: Followup:

Name:
Date: Phone: Followup:

Name:
Date: Phone: Followup:

Name:
Date: Phone: Followup:

General Notes

PROSPECTS LOG

Name:

Date: Phone: Followup:

Name:

Date: Phone: Followup:

Name:

Date: Phone: Followup:

Name:

Date: Phone: Followup:

Name:

Date: Phone: Followup:

General Notes

PROSPECTS LOG

Name:
Date: Phone: Followup:

Name:
Date: Phone: Followup:

Name:
Date: Phone: Followup:

Name:
Date: Phone: Followup:

Name:
Date: Phone: Followup:

General Notes

PROSPECTS LOG

Name:

Date: Phone: Followup:

Name:

Date: Phone: Followup:

Name:

Date: Phone: Followup:

Name:

Date: Phone: Followup:

Name:

Date: Phone: Followup:

General Notes

PROSPECTS LOG

Name:
Date: Phone: Followup:

Name:
Date: Phone: Followup:

Name:
Date: Phone: Followup:

Name:
Date: Phone: Followup:

Name:
Date: Phone: Followup:

General Notes

PROSPECTS LOG

Name:
Date: Phone: Followup:

Name:
Date: Phone: Followup:

Name:
Date: Phone: Followup:

Name:
Date: Phone: Followup:

Name:
Date: Phone: Followup:

General Notes

PROSPECTS LOG

Name:
Date: Phone: Followup:

Name:
Date: Phone: Followup:

Name:
Date: Phone: Followup:

Name:
Date: Phone: Followup:

Name:
Date: Phone: Followup:

General Notes

PROSPECTS LOG

Name:
Date: Phone: Followup:

Name:
Date: Phone: Followup:

Name:
Date: Phone: Followup:

Name:
Date: Phone: Followup:

Name:
Date: Phone: Followup:

General Notes

PROSPECTS LOG

Name:
Date: Phone: Followup:

Name:
Date: Phone: Followup:

Name:
Date: Phone: Followup:

Name:
Date: Phone: Followup:

Name:
Date: Phone: Followup:

General Notes

PROSPECTS LOG

Name:
Date: Phone: Followup:

Name:
Date: Phone: Followup:

Name:
Date: Phone: Followup:

Name:
Date: Phone: Followup:

Name:
Date: Phone: Followup:

General Notes

PROSPECTS LOG

Name:

Date: Phone: Followup:

Name:

Date: Phone: Followup:

Name:

Date: Phone: Followup:

Name:

Date: Phone: Followup:

Name:

Date: Phone: Followup:

General Notes

PROSPECTS LOG

Name:
Date: Phone: Followup:

Name:
Date: Phone: Followup:

Name:
Date: Phone: Followup:

Name:
Date: Phone: Followup:

Name:
Date: Phone: Followup:

General Notes

PROSPECTS LOG

Name:
Date: Phone: Followup:

Name:
Date: Phone: Followup:

Name:
Date: Phone: Followup:

Name:
Date: Phone: Followup:

Name:
Date: Phone: Followup:

General Notes

PROSPECTS LOG

Name:
Date: Phone: Followup:

Name:
Date: Phone: Followup:

Name:
Date: Phone: Followup:

Name:
Date: Phone: Followup:

Name:
Date: Phone: Followup:

General Notes

PROSPECTS LOG

Name:

Date: Phone: Followup:

Name:

Date: Phone: Followup:

Name:

Date: Phone: Followup:

Name:

Date: Phone: Followup:

Name:

Date: Phone: Followup:

General Notes

PROSPECTS LOG

Name:

Date: Phone: Followup:

Name:

Date: Phone: Followup:

Name:

Date: Phone: Followup:

Name:

Date: Phone: Followup:

Name:

Date: Phone: Followup:

General Notes

PROSPECTS LOG

Name:
Date: Phone: Followup:

Name:
Date: Phone: Followup:

Name:
Date: Phone: Followup:

Name:
Date: Phone: Followup:

Name:
Date: Phone: Followup:

General Notes

PROSPECTS LOG

Name:

Date: Phone: Followup:

Name:

Date: Phone: Followup:

Name:

Date: Phone: Followup:

Name:

Date: Phone: Followup:

Name:

Date: Phone: Followup:

General Notes

PROSPECTS LOG

Name:
Date: Phone: Followup:

Name:
Date: Phone: Followup:

Name:
Date: Phone: Followup:

Name:
Date: Phone: Followup:

Name:
Date: Phone: Followup:

General Notes

PROSPECTS LOG

Name:

Date: Phone: Followup:

Name:

Date: Phone: Followup:

Name:

Date: Phone: Followup:

Name:

Date: Phone: Followup:

Name:

Date: Phone: Followup:

General Notes

PROSPECTS LOG

Name:

Date: Phone: Followup:

Name:

Date: Phone: Followup:

Name:

Date: Phone: Followup:

Name:

Date: Phone: Followup:

Name:

Date: Phone: Followup:

General Notes

PROSPECTS LOG

Name:
Date: Phone: Followup:

Name:
Date: Phone: Followup:

Name:
Date: Phone: Followup:

Name:
Date: Phone: Followup:

Name:
Date: Phone: Followup:

General Notes

PROSPECTS LOG

Name:
Date: Phone: Followup:

Name:
Date: Phone: Followup:

Name:
Date: Phone: Followup:

Name:
Date: Phone: Followup:

Name:
Date: Phone: Followup:

General Notes

PROSPECTS LOG

Name:
Date: Phone: Followup:

Name:
Date: Phone: Followup:

Name:
Date: Phone: Followup:

Name:
Date: Phone: Followup:

Name:
Date: Phone: Followup:

General Notes

PROSPECTS LOG

Name:

Date: Phone: Followup:

Name:

Date: Phone: Followup:

Name:

Date: Phone: Followup:

Name:

Date: Phone: Followup:

Name:

Date: Phone: Followup:

General Notes

PROSPECTS LOG

Name:

Date: Phone: Followup:

Name:

Date: Phone: Followup:

Name:

Date: Phone: Followup:

Name:

Date: Phone: Followup:

Name:

Date: Phone: Followup:

General Notes

PROSPECTS LOG

Name:
Date: Phone: Followup:

Name:
Date: Phone: Followup:

Name:
Date: Phone: Followup:

Name:
Date: Phone: Followup:

Name:
Date: Phone: Followup:

General Notes

PROSPECTS LOG

Name:
Date: Phone: Followup:

Name:
Date: Phone: Followup:

Name:
Date: Phone: Followup:

Name:
Date: Phone: Followup:

Name:
Date: Phone: Followup:

General Notes

PROSPECTS LOG

Name:
Date: Phone: Followup:

Name:
Date: Phone: Followup:

Name:
Date: Phone: Followup:

Name:
Date: Phone: Followup:

Name:
Date: Phone: Followup:

General Notes

PROSPECTS LOG

Name:
Date: Phone: Followup:

Name:
Date: Phone: Followup:

Name:
Date: Phone: Followup:

Name:
Date: Phone: Followup:

Name:
Date: Phone: Followup:

General Notes

PROSPECTS LOG

Name:
Date: Phone: Followup:

Name:
Date: Phone: Followup:

Name:
Date: Phone: Followup:

Name:
Date: Phone: Followup:

Name:
Date: Phone: Followup:

Made in the USA
Coppell, TX
05 March 2022

74448519R00068